Fact Finders®

PERSPECTIVES ON HISTORY

ANDREW JACKSON

HEROIC LEADER OR COLD-HEARTED RULER?

by Nel Yomtov

Consultant:
Richard Bell
Associate Professor of History
University of Maryland, College Park

CAPSTONE PRESS
a capstone imprint

Fact Finders Books are published by Capstone Press,
1710 Roe Crest Drive, North Mankato, Minnesota 56003
www.capstonepub.com

Library of Congress Cataloging-in-Publication Data
Yomtov, Nel.
Andrew Jackson : heroic leader or cold-hearted ruler? / by Nel Yomtov.
pages cm. — (Fact finders. Perspectives on History)
Summary: "Describes Andrew Jackson's actions during the War of 1812 and the Trail of Tears"—
Provided by publisher.
Includes bibliographical references and index.
ISBN 978-1-4765-0245-8 (library binding)
ISBN 978-1-4765-3409-1 (paperback)
ISBN 978-1-4765-3417-6 (ebook PDF)
1. Jackson, Andrew, 1767–1845—Juvenile literature. 2. Presidents—United States—Biography—
Juvenile literature. I. Title.
E382.Y66 2014
973.5'6092—dc23
[B]   2013003357

Editorial Credits
Mari Bolte, editor; Ted Williams, designer; Svetlana Zhurkin, media researcher;
Laura Manthe, production specialist

Photo Credits
Library of Congress, cover (middle right), 5, 9, 16, 18 (top), 26, 29; Newscom: Everett Collection,
15, Picture History, cover (bottom left), 25; North Wind Picture Archives, 7, 11, 12, 22; Shutterstock:
2happy, cover (background), Alena Hovorkova (design elements), throughout, Dianka Pyzhova
(design elements), throughout, exshutter (vintage paper sheet), 7 and throughout, Oleksiy Fedorov
(background texture), throughout

Direct Quotes
p. 4 from President Andrew Jackson's Message to Congress "On Indian Removal," December 6,
1830. Records of the United States Senate, 1789–1990. (http://www.archives.gov/historical-docs/
todays-doc/?dod-date=1206)
p. 13 from Publications of the Southern History Association, Volume 2 (Washington, D.C.: Southern
History Association, 1897–1907)
p. 23 from Andrew Jackson: "First Annual Message," December 8, 1829
(http://www.presidency.ucsb.edu/ws/?pid=29471)
p. 27 from Transcript of President Andrew Jackson's Message to Congress: "On Indian Removal,"
December 6, 1830 (http://www.ourdocuments.gov/doc.php?flash=true&doc=25)
p. 27 (fact box) from Andrew Jackson: "To the Cherokee Tribe of Indians East of the Mississippi,"
March 16, 1835 (http://www.gilderlehrman.org/history-by-era/jackson-lincoln/resources/
andrew-jackson-cherokee-tribe-1835)

Printed in the United States of America in Brainerd, Minnesota.
032013   007721BANGF13

TABLE OF CONTENTS

A Complex Man

On December 6, 1830, President Andrew Jackson addressed the members of Congress. He boldly spoke about the fate of American Indians. He said,

"The kind policy of the government in relation to the removal of the Indians ... is approaching a happy ending. It will separate the Indians from immediate contact with settlements of whites ... and perhaps cause them gradually to cast off their savage habits and become an interesting, civilized community."

To modern readers Jackson's words may seem harsh and insensitive. Yet history shows that Jackson was a complex man. Some people say he was friendly and caring. Jackson was an accomplished serviceman and one of America's greatest military heroes. Others say he was a mean-spirited, cruel **tyrant**. Some claim he was murderous, especially in his treatment of American Indians.

What is the truth? Who is the real Andrew Jackson? Take a look at the life of this unique American and decide for yourself.

Andrew Jackson became the seventh president of the United States.

tyrant: someone who rules other people in a cruel or unjust way

Chapter 1

SURVIVING THE FRONTIER

Andrew Jackson was born on March 15, 1767. He grew up in the Waxhaws, a **frontier** region of the Catawba River valley. His home was near the border between the British **colonies** in North and South Carolina.

Early life was difficult for the young Jackson. He grew up without a father. Andrew Jackson Sr. had died months before the birth of his third son. Jackson's mother moved in with her brother-in-law's family. She would be their maid. In exchange the two younger Jackson boys could live there too.

The Waxhaws was good farm country. But constant wars between white settlers and Cherokee Indians had largely destroyed the region. Crime and violence ran wild. People feared for their lives and property.

frontier: the far edge of a country, where few people live

colony: a place that is settled by people from another country and is controlled by that country

Jackson was a stubborn and angry youngster. He had a bad temper that he often could not control. The smallest things made him upset. He was always feeling a need to prove himself. He liked to play pranks and was often in trouble. One of his uncle's slaves called him the "most mischievous of youngsters" in the region.

a settler family and their log cabin in the Carolinas

FACT

Young Andrew Jackson preferred outdoor activities to school lessons and reading books. He was a skilled horseback rider and racer. As president he kept racehorses in the White House stables.

The Revolutionary War (1775–1783) forced young Jackson to grow up quickly. By 1779 fighting had reached the Carolinas. Jackson helped his mother care for wounded soldiers in the local church. His 16-year-old brother, Hugh, rode off to fight. Hugh died while defending Charleston, South Carolina. There was chaos and confusion throughout the region. Many settlers fled to seek safety.

Jackson strongly supported the American cause for freedom. In 1780 he and his brother Robert joined the South Carolina **militia**. The Jackson brothers were captured by British soldiers the next spring. While captive, Andrew refused to clean the boots of a British officer. The soldier slashed the youngster's face and hands with a sword. The brothers were sent to prison. There, they became ill with **smallpox**.

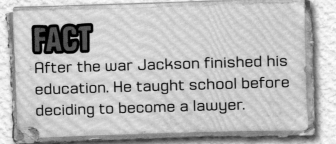

FACT

After the war Jackson finished his education. He taught school before deciding to become a lawyer.

milita: a group of people who are trained to fight but are not professional soldiers

smallpox: a contagious disease

Jackson's mother begged for her sons' freedom. An officer agreed to trade the boys for captive British soldiers. Days after they returned home, however, Robert died. Weeks later his mother died while caring for Patriot soldiers in Charleston. Fourteen-year-old Andrew was alone.

"Brave Boy of the Waxhaws" shows 14-year-old Jackson being punished by a British officer.

Chapter 2

A CLASH OF CULTURES

The Revolutionary War ended in 1783. By 1788 Jackson had become a lawyer and settled in Nashville, Tennessee. Bloody battles between whites and American Indians were common in the area. Like most settlers Jackson thought of Indians as savages. He also believed they should not have any property rights. They were too violent to live next to whites.

Growing up Jackson had heard tales of Waxhaws settlers fighting off Indian attacks. He believed that one day he would have to wage war against the Indian "enemy." In his mind Indians represented madness and disorder. They reminded him of a childhood that he wanted to forget.

American Indians attacked settlers who lived close to their homelands.

settlers in Tennessee around 1800

After arriving in Nashville, Jackson joined a local military group as a scout and a fighter. The group attacked Cherokee Indians who raided a white settlement. The Cherokees were angry because whites had broken several **treaties** with them. The treaties had recognized Indian independence. They also guaranteed the Indians land to live on peacefully. White settlers did not observe treaties. They kept moving into Cherokee lands. Then they would demand a new treaty, which they broke again.

Jackson supported the settlers. Like most whites Jackson believed that America belonged to the white man. Only whites should be able to develop and control the land. The Indians stood in the way of success. Jackson would do anything to remove the Indians.

treaty: an official agreement between two or more groups or countries

AN OPPONENT OF PEACE TREATIES

Jackson opposed politicians who wanted to peacefully settle with Indians. In 1794 he wrote, "... Treaties answer no other purpose than opening an easy door for the Indians to pass through to butcher our citizens." Jackson also wanted harsh punishments for "the Barbarians for murdering ... innocent citizens."

Chapter 3

WAGING WAR UPON HIS ENEMIES

By 1803 the ambitious Jackson had become a judge in Tennessee. He was also a major general in the state militia. He opened stores, owned a farm, and sold land and slaves. He was becoming a popular, wealthy man with big political and military goals.

Jackson found the opportunity for military fame during the War of 1812 (1812–1815). The war was fought between the United States and Great Britain. Another fight, called the Creek War (1813–1814), was also taking place within the Creek nation.

In August 1813, a group of Creek Indians called the Red Sticks attacked Fort Mims in Alabama. They **massacred** white settlers and mixed-blood Creeks who lived there. Because Red Sticks were British **allies**, Tennessee's governor ordered Jackson to strike back. Jackson's army of 5,000 white men and Choctaw Indians obeyed. They brutally killed Red Stick warriors, women, and children.

The Battle of Fort Mims lasted about three hours. Nearly 250 people inside the fort were killed.

Jackson's victories over the Creek gave him national fame. He was named brigadier general in the U.S. Army. He was put in command of the entire Gulf of Mexico region. He also became known as a ruthless killer.

massacre: to needlessly kill a group of helpless people

allies: people who are on the same side during a war

Jackson dealt a final blow to the Red Sticks in 1814. His army cornered them at the Horse Shoe Bend of the Tallapoosa River in Alabama. Jackson's soldiers shot many Indians as they tried to escape into the river. Those who lagged behind were drowned. More than 900 Red Sticks died. Around 300 were taken prisoner. Most of the captives were women and children. In August Jackson met with the Creek leaders. He forced them to sign a treaty. The treaty forced them to give more than half of their land to the U.S. government.

Jackson with Creek leader William Weatherford (also known as Red Eagle)

The treaty, known as the Treaty of Fort Jackson, ended the Creek War. It also added 23 million acres (9.3 million hectares) to the United States. The land was fertile and perfect for plantation farming.

The Creeks were required to allow the building of U.S. military posts, trading points, and roads throughout the territory. The Creeks were also forbidden to have contact with British or Spanish traders.

Meanwhile, runaway black slaves from Georgia were fleeing into Spanish-owned Florida. The slaves were often protected by the Seminole Indians who lived there. President James Monroe wished to end border conflicts between slave owners and the Indians. He ordered Jackson's troops to attack the Seminoles. The troops were to follow the Indians into Florida if necessary. But they were not to attack if the Seminoles sought safety in a Spanish fort.

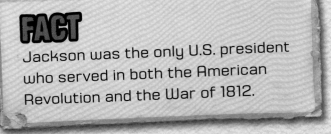

FACT

Jackson was the only U.S. president who served in both the American Revolution and the War of 1812.

Jackson's victory during the Battle of New Orleans in 1815 made him a national hero.

the locations of Jackson's military victories

WEST VIRGINIA

VIRGINIA

KENTUCKY

NORTH CAROLINA

TENNESSEE

ARKANSAS

SOUTH CAROLINA

Horse Shoe Bend

GEORGIA

ALABAMA

LOUISIANA

Fort Mims

MISSISSIPPI

FLORIDA

Pensacola

Battle of New Orleans

N W E S

The War of 1812 ended in 1815. But another was about to begin. The conflicts between the U.S. Army and the Seminoles started the First Seminole War (1817–1818). In March 1818 Jackson entered Florida. He destroyed several Seminole towns. Ignoring Monroe's orders, he captured a Spanish fort. Runaway slaves and Indians had been storing weapons in the fort. He **executed** two British men judged guilty of aiding the Indians. He also executed two Indian leaders.

Weeks later Jackson captured the nearby Spanish-held town of Pensacola. Despite disobeying orders, Jackson had gained control of Spanish Florida. In February 1819 Spain sold Florida to the United States. Many people viewed Jackson as a hero.

President Monroe put Jackson in charge of the Indians' fate. He made Jackson his main treaty **negotiator**. He was in charge of setting up a government in Florida. His victory also freed the United States from a large debt to Spain.

execute: to put to death

negotiator: someone who reaches an agreement by discussing something

Chapter 4

THE TRAIL OF TEARS

Jackson was a tough treaty negotiator. Between 1814 and 1824, he negotiated nine treaties. These treaties turned Indian territories into government land. Jackson often allowed his friends to buy land given up by the Indians.

Jackson wanted to bring American Indians under government control. He thought they should not be allowed to follow their tribal laws. Instead, the government would protect them. The Indians would no longer have to worry about hostile tribes and white men on Indian lands.

INDIAN TERRITORY

In 1803 the United States bought 828,000 square miles (2.1 million square kilometers) of land from France. The deal was called the Louisiana Purchase. The land made up all or part of 15 current U.S. states. It also included the Mississippi River. Jackson believed this territory could be a home for all eastern Indians.

In 1820 Jackson met with Choctaw Indians in Mississippi. He told them that they had to move west if they wished to hold on to their culture. If they did not accept his offer, he said their nation "would be destroyed." Many Choctaws moved to Indian Territory. They also gave up a vast amount of valuable land to the U.S. government.

HOW MUCH LAND DID THE INDIANS GET?

This map shows the land gained by the United States during the Louisiana Purchase. It also shows the original locations of the eastern tribes. The purple area is the land set aside for the tribes during the Indian Removal Act.

Jackson had found his fame. In 1828 he was elected the seventh president of the United States. By this time, there were about 65,000 Indians living in the Southeast. They were called the "Five Civilized Tribes." They included Cherokees, Creeks, Seminoles, Chickasaws, and the remaining Choctaws. They were the largest group of native peoples living in the United States.

Many of these people had adopted white culture. They learned how to farm and trade. Many had built plantations and trading posts. Christian missionaries had taught them to read and write. Many tribes had also set up schools, churches, and newspapers.

In 1823 the Supreme Court ruled that American Indians could live in the United States. But they could not own any land.

But white farmers wanted these Indian lands. The lands could grow cotton and held other valuable resources. Jackson saw this as an opportunity to move American Indians into Indian Territory. In December 1829 he asked Congress to set aside land there. He also found funds to remove the Indians from the East. In 1830 Congress passed the Indian Removal Act. It was a close vote. Many congressmen opposed Jackson's policy. They thought it was harsh and unfair.

WHAT DID HE REALLY MEAN?

In a speech to Congress in 1829, President Jackson said that the "emigration should be voluntary, for it would be as cruel as unjust to compel the [Indians] to abandon the graves of their fathers and seek a home in a distant land." However, even before his election Jackson had been set on forcing Indians off their lands. One of his first actions after becoming president was to sign the Indian Removal Act.

emigration: the act of leaving one region or country to settle in another

The forced **migration** of Indians into present-day Oklahoma lasted several years. From 1831 to 1832, about 23,000 Choctaws and Cherokees were moved. At first the Cherokees refused to leave. But 15,000 were eventually forced from their homes. Soldiers gathered them into groups and herded them west. The Alabama Creeks were moved in 1836. Chickasaws went the following year.

The brutal 800-mile (1,300-kilometer) trek became known as the "Trail of Tears." The Indians were not allowed to pack or bring things from their homes. Many were put in military camps. Hundreds died as prisoners.

Freezing winters and extremely hot summers killed many. The weak or sick were left to die. Many Indians were put on steamboats for part of the journey. They were boxed into cramped railroad cars like animals. Overcrowded boats also caused deadly accidents on the river ways.

The food given to the Indians was usually spoiled or rotten. Much of it was considered unfit to be eaten by whites. The drinking water was dirty. Those who tried to flee were rounded up and put in chains.

By 1837 about one-third of all eastern Indians had died because of the Removal Act. More than one-fourth of the Cherokee nation died. By 1860 there were fewer than 300,000 Indians left in America—and more than 30 million white people.

THE TRAIL OF TEARS
by Robert Lindneux

This painting was done in 1942. It shows the suffering of the Cherokee people during the Trail of Tears. In reality, only the very rich or the very sick and old rode. The rest were forced to walk.

migration: the act of moving from one area or country to another

History Judges Andrew Jackson

We may never know Jackson's true motives on Indian Removal. Some historians say he wanted to create a new Indian society. The Indian warrior would be turned into a peaceful farmer who adopted white culture. Others say his removal policy was necessary to preserve Indian culture. The only way to do this was to separate whites and Indians forever.

Jackson himself claimed he was the Indians' friend and protector. He even referred to them as "my red children." He could not understand why tribes resisted his removal policy. He felt he was offering them a safe new home away from white civilization. "How many thousands of our own people would gladly embrace the opportunity!" he wondered.

FACT

In a letter to Cherokee leaders urging them to move west, Jackson said, "I have no motive, my friends, to **deceive** you. I am sincerely desirous to promote your welfare." The Cherokees ignored his offer. Jackson sent government agents to force the Cherokees from their homeland.

deceive: to trick someone into believing something that is not true

Other people believe Jackson's policies were harsh and anti-Indian. He had brutally crushed Indians in the Creek and Seminole Wars. He frequently ignored treaties and illegally took land away from Indians.

Experts also wonder how realistic Jackson's fatherly attitude was toward the Indians. He strongly believed America should expand across the continent. Did he truly think that his removal policy would protect Indians from whites? Surely he could have predicted the terrible fate for his Indian "children." Whites had proven over and over that they would stop at nothing to take Indian lands.

There are no simple answers to help define Andrew Jackson's actions. Over time, the images of Jackson as a polite and caring war hero or an evil villain have faded. Historians now hold more complex viewpoints of him.

So, was Andrew Jackson a hero or a villain? What do you think?

Jackson's troops called him "Old Hickory." The Cherokee Indians called him "Sharp Knife."

GLOSSARY

allies (AL-eyes)—people who are on the same side during a war

colony (KAH-luh-nee)—a place that is settled by people from another country and is controlled by that country

deceive (di-SEEV)—to trick someone into believing something that is not true

emigration (em-i-GRAY-shuhn)—the act of leaving one region or country to settle in another

execute (EK-si-kyoot)—to put to death

frontier (fruhn-TEER)—the far edge of a country, where few people live

massacre (MASS-uh-kuhr)—to needlessly kill a group of helpless people

migration (mye-GRAY-shuhn)—the act of moving from one area or country to another

militia (muh-LISH-uh)—a group of people who are trained to fight but are not professional soldiers

negotiator (ni-GOH-shee-ay-tur)—someone who reaches an agreement by discussing something

smallpox (SMAWL-pahks)—a contagious disease that causes a rash, high fever, and blisters

treaty (TREE-tee)—an official agreement between two or more groups or countries

tyrant (TYE-ruhnt)—someone who rules other people in a cruel or unjust way

READ MORE

Benoit, Peter. *The Trail of Tears.* Cornerstones of Freedom. New York: Children's Press, 2012.

Josephson, Judith Pinkerton. *Why Did Cherokees Move West?: And Other Questions about the Trail of Tears.* Six Questions of American History. Minneapolis: Lerner Publications, 2011.

Marsico, Katie. *Andrew Jackson.* Presidents and Their Times. New York: Marshall Cavendish Benchmark, 2011.

INTERNET SITES

FactHound offers a safe, fun way to find Internet sites related to this book. All of the sites on FactHound have been researched by our staff.

Here's all you do:
Visit *www.facthound.com*
Type in this code: 9781476502458

Check out projects, games and lots more at
www.capstonekids.com

CRITICAL THINKING USING THE COMMON CORE

1. During his life, Andrew Jackson's opinion of American Indians changed drastically. Describe his opinion at a young age and tell how his opinion changed. What led to his shift in attitude? Use details from the text to support your answer. (Key Ideas and Details)

2. Andrew Jackson believed that the land acquired from the Louisiana Purchase could be set aside for Indians. Take a close look at the map on page 21. Contrast the amount of land gained by the Louisiana Purchase with the amount of land the Indians actually received. (Craft and Structure)

3. Imagine Congress had not passed the Indian Removal Act. How might the United States be different today? (Integration of Knowledge and Ideas)

INDEX